Sport is Fun

Dianne Irving

Contents

Sport	2
Football	4
Swimming	6
Running	8
Cricket	10
Picture Index	12

Sport

We like to play sport.

Football

Football is fun.
I like football a lot.

I kick the ball.
I hit the net!

Swimming

It is fun to swim.
I like it a lot.

I get into the pool.
I kick my legs.

Running

Running is fun.
I like to run.

I can run and run.
I am good at it!

Cricket

Cricket is fun.
I like cricket.

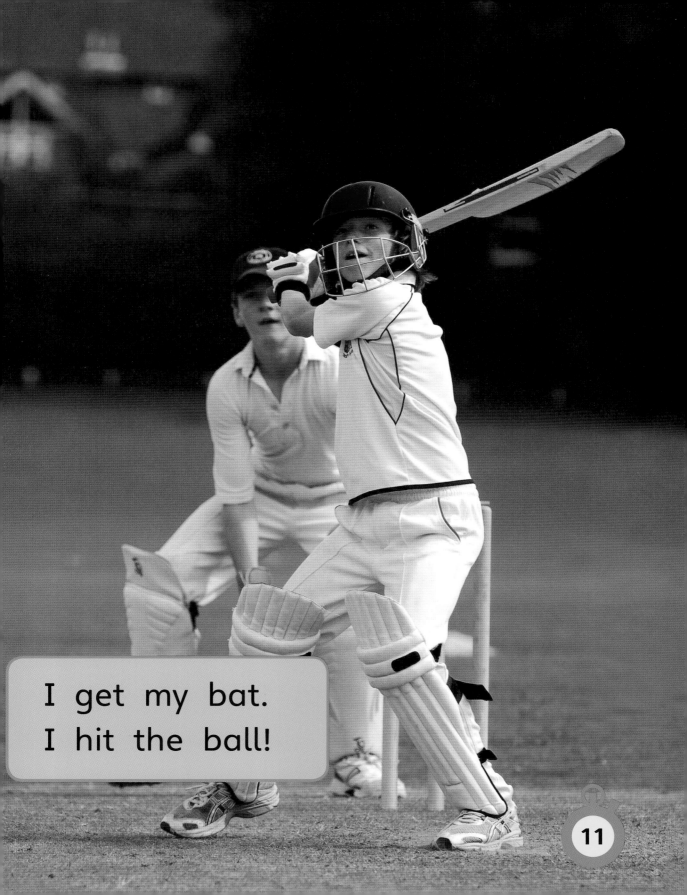

I get my bat.
I hit the ball!

Picture Index

 cricket 10–11

 football 4–5

 running 8–9

 swimming 6–7